Questionable Views

poems by

Ed Ahern

Finishing Line Press
Georgetown, Kentucky

Questionable Views

Copyright © 2023 by Ed Ahern
ISBN 979-8-88838-260-8 First Edition
All rights reserved under International and Pan-American Copyright Conventions. No part of this book may be reproduced in any manner whatsoever without written permission from the publisher, except in the case of brief quotations embodied in critical articles and reviews.

ACKNOWLEDGMENTS

Deepfelt thanks are due to the publications who first accepted each poem. They are:

Title	First Published
Sensual Living	Seventh Quarry
Musical Melee	Cerasus
The Lock Out	Fresh Words
Covid Largesse	New Verse News
Words for a Full-Fledged Kestrel	Academy of Hearts and Minds
City Viewpoints	Bombfire
Gleaning the Attic	Vita Brevis
An Elegy for Silent Letters	Continue the Voice
Last Man Standing	Amsterdam Quarterly
The Engagement Present	Enjoy Radio (UK)
Compared to What	Across the Margins
Peep Show	Verse Virtual
Death and Scaling	Ephemeral Elegies
The School Outing	Pure Slush
The Time of Day	Red Eft
Absence	One Art Poetry
French Cuffed	Brown Bag
We Lepers	Bewildering Stories
Visit to an Unmarked Grave	Southwest Poetry Review
Trick or Treat	Sage Cigarettes
Fire Tending	Glow
Which I Am	October Hill
Insatiable	Verse Virtual
Seasoned Moments	Bloom
Gustavo's Rite	As Above So Below

Publisher: Leah Huete de Maines
Editor: Christen Kincaid
Cover Art: Daniel Spose
Author Photo: Elizabeth Ahern
Cover Design: Elizabeth Maines McCleavy

Order online: www.finishinglinepress.com and amazon.com

Author inquiries and mail orders:
Finishing Line Press
PO Box 1626
Georgetown, Kentucky 40324
USA

Table of Contents

Sensual Living 1

Musical Melee 2

The Lock Out 3

Covid Largesse 4

Words for a Full-Fledged Kestrel 5

City Viewpoints 6

Gleaning the Attic 7

An Elegy for Silent Letters 8

Last Man Standing 9

The Engagement Present 10

Compared to What 11

Peep Show 12

Death and Scaling 13

The School Outing 15

The Time of Day 17

Absence 18

French Cuffed 19

We Lepers 20

Visit to an Unmarked Grave 21

Trick or Treat 22

Fire Tending 23

Which I Am 24

Insatiable 25

Seasoned Moments 26

Gustavo's Rite 27

Sensual Living

To my eyes light is or is not,
my ears hear or don't hear you,
I can or can't smell sweetness or rot,
I am touched or not touched,
taste is missing or savored.

But river eagles see through water
Bat ears sense moth wings
A distant vulture smells the dead
A monarch drinks just milkweed
And cat whiskers graze the unknown

Science tells us light has speed
But does it slow as it curves?
At how few parts per million does
infinitesimal odor become the undetectable?
Could we ever hear the world breathing?

To failingly understand these things
My senses are kidnapped into thoughts
unfelt, unsmelled, unseen, unheard, and tasteless.
And well beyond my grasp.
I accept science on faith.

Musical Melee

One hot summer evening in a city,
Stripped off clothing, open windows.
Traffic stopped for cross-walkers
at the street corner of sound Babel.
Musics punched each other for place.
car raps wrestled with window gospels,
ped speakers shoved rock against bachata,
and classical whimpered in the undersound.
The round ended with traffic light change
And the musics moved to neutral corners.

The Lock Out

I know a man who has hated me
for almost twenty years.
For reasons important to another
I've tried and failed to create
a neutrality that allows for us
to coexist socially.

Of what I did there is no doubt
and his repugnance has held firm.
The clenched endurance of his hate
speaks perhaps to the gravity
of my offense, or perhaps
to his emotional intransigence.

In either case I was one with
several others whom he hates
with equal vigor and longevity,
and sometimes for less reason.
Such unyielding hate is powerful
but I suspect not comforting.

Covid Largesse

Aesop got it wrong.
Or at least incomplete.
This life-long ant realizes
some of my money will outlive me.
And here comes a Covid check.
More for the kids? Not likely.
But how to best squander it?
I'm too old for expensive vices,
and already giving things away.
Spas and salons are wasted
on a wrinkled, bald man.
What's left is geriatric dissipation.
Grasshopper trips and meals,
shows and concerts,
gorged on at sedate pace,
with lessened senses and focus
and an age restricted diet.

Words for a Full-fledged Kestrel

You've done really well with
the first quarter of your life.
Now comes the interesting parts,
the ones with no refunds.

You'll undoubtedly fail at some things
and make mistakes even when succeeding.
Just treat it all like a Sunday dinner
and eat everything on your plate.

We old insist on offering
you young weathered advice
on safe passage through life
which you can safely ignore

How we lived, what we did
are well recorded and extinct.
Pretensions we thought important
are on sale at Good Will.

Protect your sense of purposeless fun
and tolerate your minor absurdities,
for achievements go stale after their creation,
and difficulties always dwindle into nuisances.

Who you are and what you want
will change as you discover yourself.
Just keep your sense of wonder close
and sense of humor closer.

Remember to enjoy the trip.

With Great Love,
Granddad Ahern

City Viewpoints

The view from planes is pin hole camera
looking down onto topographic miniature.
The view from trains is ass-ended humanity,
factory loading docks and backyard dumps.
The view from limos is sly voyeuristic,
tinted glass shielding leers and gawks.
But the view from buses is curdling,
street corner trash and sullen walkers,
glares of anger and annoyance,
blares of clotted traffic, all while
cramp-seated in rear toilet miasma.

Gleaning the Attic

The purgatory of my possessions
reproaches me from the jumbled attic.
Dusty sleeping bags and thermal wear
cached for trips no longer taken.
Books on fishing and philosophy
long unnibbled except by paper lice.
An oversized, silver-plated tea service,
a present from a long-gone aunt,
blackened from never once being used.
Phonograph records from a dead mother
Not played in several decades.
A concretion of things once treasured,
lacking any present grace or purpose,
hoping to be redeemed by new owners.

An Elegy for Silent Letters

Logic**a**lly, if a letter's in a word
Succum**b**ing to silence isn't an option.
Obs**c**ene elisions should never occur
E**d**ges or middle, stressed or soft
Lov**e** of aspiration should be taught.
Champa**g**ne poured for enunciation.
Ghost letters, however, abound.
Business coddles brevity.
Knives are taken to sounds.
Fo**l**k refuse stutter steps.
Dam**n** it all let's be precise.

Last Man Standing

Man is the last species to die,
for he can eat all the others.
Plankton, plant, pork or porgy
All go down his maw.
Forget about cockroaches and rats,
Man dines on them both.
Consider seafood as example.
Poisonous blowfish,
mercury-laced lampreys,
sea urchins and periwinkles,
sharks and slugs and squid,
even rotted, all eaten.
And after man consumes
all the plants and animals
he's apt to eat other men.

The Engagement Present

A half century ago I bought my engagement present.
Not the one I gave her, but the one she gave me.
I don't recall ever asking her to pay for it.
The gold plated Bulova Acutron watch
lasted through several watch straps but finally,
despite a couple of new batteries, declined to run.
There are only two places in North America
that are willing to repair it, and both charge
five times its purchase price to do so.
And if I paid for the repair it would be worth
less than half of the cost to fix it
 The watch is coffined in my jewelry case
since I cannot let myself discard it,
and I wonder if I should put it back on
simply as male wrist ornamentation
for I cannot remember the last occasion
someone has asked me for the time.

Compared to What

Life is sliding down the flat of a knife blade
while it's being randomly waved,
and hoping not to slip into its sharpness.
I've never undergone a worst day-
bad and often cringeworthy of course,
but never irretrievably maiming.
We've had a miscarriage, but healthy children;
I've lost jobs but always found another;
been broken and scarred but always healed;
been bitterly disappointed in some,
but found many others who held true.
Feared that I'd failed myself,
but always found little successes,
feet set on the oiled blade.

Peep Show

In rare, random, wordless moments
I can glimpse the rightness of things,
the glamour of a beetle on a weed,
the chest-seizing love for a child,
the taste without taste of cool water.

The over rushing glow is an instant,
the afterglow perhaps a minute.
But in that flicker I am at peace.
A satori of seconds? A transient nirvana?
In this interlude I neither know nor care

Death and Scaling

I encountered death at eight.
Not people death, that happened at ten.
Fish death, and autopsy, and undertaking.

My grandmother, a petit but wiry thing,
would knead leftover oatmeal into balls.
These I gently inserted into a minnow trap,
walked it down the dock and lowered away.
Minnows entered and ate their last meal.

They were hauled out of the water,
flopping against wire until being poured
into a concrete holding tank, then later
netted into a bucket and put into a boat
my grandmother and I went fishing in.

She showed me how to put the hook
through the muscle behind their head,
crippling the minnow but not killing it,
and would scold me if I killed one
before it could enter a perch's mouth
and be swallowed deep enough
for the hook to set in the perch's throat.

Ten minnows would die in the bucket
before being offered up the food chain.
Two thirds were mouth mangled by perch,
the rest dumped in the lake, too sickly
to survive another trip to the holding tank.
The bucket would be refilled with water
and perhaps twenty just-dead perch.
Enough to feed our family.

We returned at dusk, too late for cleaning.
The bucket went into well house water
so cold it hurt our teeth to drink,
until the next morning before breakfast, when
I arrived bleary eyed with knife and scaler
to perform surgery on stiff corpses
in an aproned, ordained way.

Slice the head almost off, then
keeping the knife in place slice
down the belly to the anus.
Grasp the head and pull out the guts.
Lop off the tail and slice down the back
just left of the dorsal fins, then
slice right and pull out the back fins.

Then slice off the pelvic and anal fins.
Then scraper time, both flanks, diligently.
My hands and the front of my apron
glitter coated with slime sticky scales
rinse off with a hose, and again, and again

Then cut out the backbone and filet out
the tiny rib bones that could catch
in our throats while eating.
Then quality control, any flaws sternly rejected
and requiring a recleaning.

The little pearly slabs were delivered
to the refrigerator and I would try and fail
to scrub away the smells of slime and guts.
Twice a week, all summer for several years.
One of my fondest memories.

The School Outing

This admission serves as confession,
for I will never reveal it to a priest.
The transgression occurred after graduating
from St. Eulalia elementary school.
(Virgin and martyr, AD 303. Maybe.
There is uncertainty about
where and when she existed,
or if she existed at all.)

A friend and I exited Sunday mass.
We wandered down a corridor
to a little used door that connected
the Church to adjoining school.
The door, for unknown reason
was left unlocked and we entered.
We walked aimlessly, absorbing
three-month-old nostalgia.

Until reaching the Lost and Found.
The pitiful lock was penknife picked
and we found Ali Baba's treasure,
generations of unclaimed marvels.
Fountain pens and mechanical pencils,
scarves and lunch boxes and rulers,
pins and watches and even rings.
And a tray full of skeleton keys.

As we strained our pockets in theft
we wondered if the keys might open
all those locked classroom doors.
And, miracle of evil, they did.
Those 1920's locks giving entry
into library and classrooms alike.
Except for Mother Superior's office
which had a stern looking Yale cylinder.

We jumbled books and spilled milk money,
left rude messages on blackboards,
and relocked doors behind us as we left,
unencountered and unseen.
We heard rumors of the later uproar;
current students were interrogated,
and accusations hurled at some,
but graduates were left alone.

I feared to use the pens and key chains
lest they be recognized as pillaged,
and one evening buried them all
in a neighbor's back yard garden,
to perhaps be discovered
by one more innocent than I,
who wondered at antiques in a tin box.
It was my unatoned, unexpiated crime.

The Time of Day

A widow walks by my house each day
in syncopation with the mailman.
She has also lost a daughter,
but what is gone is carried deep,
for she always smiles and stops to chat.
We exchange perhaps two hundred words
about weather and children and neighbors,
but never about the death and absence
so twined into our daily living,
and the knitting we do to cope.
We sense with tacit understanding
that our inanities give unsaid comfort
to our silenced fears and grief.

Absence

In this time of needed absence
When distant words are thin soup
And images cannot be grasped
We offer this lack of ourselves
As a protective prayer for those
We love too much to touch.
And hope that our denial
Of those we hold most close
Keeps us intact and caring
For a later day.

French Cuffed

When I first went corporate
Executives wore dress shirts
With French cuffs and gold links.
So for protective coloration
I scrounged the lower east side
For remainders from Madison Avenue.

The quality of the shirts
Improved with my credit rating
And in time my closet held
A half-month of French cuffs.
Eventually, with retirement,
The need for dressing up
Left with my commute.

Weddings, funerals and church services
Don't satisfy this need for ostentation,
And I find myself gold cuffed
At televised operas and poetry readings
I am addicted to my camouflage

We Lepers

Shared sickness creates a cure
that the healthy cannot know.
The showing of our open sores
repels those who are whole,
or who think they are.

But by admitting our diseases
to another with our sufferings
we apply cleansing words
to wash each other's defects
and rinse away the fester.

These wounds of our creation,
never apparent, always present,
cannot be removed but can
be accepted as what we were
and not as what we're becoming.

Visit to an Unmarked Grave

A while ago this friend died alone.
Maybe drunk, maybe deliberately.
No one visited him for three weeks,
so he rotted on a sofa.

We shared a secretive calling,
close friends and interests
and a serious dependency,
but not his dying.

His lived distantly enough
from my life that I doled out
help and companionship
as the occasions arose.

At the end, he'd run out of
money, health and work.
Unable to remake his life,
he brought it to a close.

His sister said good riddance
and his debtors complained,
but we few knew the man
inside the flaws and mourned.

Trick or Treat

Some experiences are inevitable-
parents, race, plumbing, talents.
Some experiences are chosen-
spouses, jobs, vices, friends.

Some sensations are virgin births-
Hunger, chill, pain, touch.
Some sensations are sought-
Warmth, comfort, exertion, enjoyment,

Some emotions are uncontrollable-
Fear, sex, laughter, wonder
Some emotions are nurtured-
Affection, honor, hate, pleasure
And some emotions are deceivers-
Lust, greed, envy, pride.

Some of this and some of that,
tricks and treats consumed
during the walk.

Fire Tending

There are rare individuals.
their hearth fire radiance
drawing me to their warmth,
thrown off without demands
for attention or favor.
I bask in the unmetered glow
of their unselfish self-focus,
rest in the calmness
of their illuminated inner unity.
I'm don't envy their shimmer,
just help them gently radiate-
not advice or instruction,
but healing perspective

Which I Am

I am the shore-bound wind
blowing sand back into the sea,
the faltering light that dries
standing water between rain storms,
the weeds that sprawl so obnoxiously
that they are cut down and burnt,
the possums that sneak out at night
and are savaged by feral dogs.
I am all of this, and am somehow
content with the process.

Insatiable

The shadowed corners
of my granted wishes
leach into my next desires.
Completeness exists
in birth and death
and maybe love,
but otherwise I find
a cavity in
every golden apple.

Seasoned Moments

Old Age is pointillism of experience
Vibrant on a graying canvas
Moments of self-illumination
Shining like a Russian icon
Atop drab robes.
The weathered revel in instants.

Gustavo's Rite

He walked onto the harbor beach at sunset,
planting a small net on a pole like a guidon,
and setting soiled cloth bags around it.
Alone on the beach he began his dance.
Mismatched clothes flapping, he swayed,
then paced, then crouched to pat the sand
into a crescent, then stepped back and back,
dug sand by hand, finding black things
and tossing them into a jumbled pile .
He stepped easily, as if riding waves,
moving in erose shapes only he knew.
Then he gathered net and bags and left,
not glancing back at the cairn
of burnt wood and asphalt fragments.

All this I watched from a restaurant deck,
and had to ask the waiter about him.
"Gustavo," he said, shrugging, "a local character."
I nodded but kept silent, recalling that morning
walking another beach, trying to feel profound.

Ed Ahern started writing fiction at sixty-seven, and poetry at seventy. He sometimes detours into literary fiction but is best known as an innovative genre writer and poet. He's tucked away several awards and honorable mentions for four hundred fifty published short stories and poems, and six books. They've appeared 800 times in ten countries and, counting reprints, over two hundred publications. Several of his stories can be listened to through Audible.

In addition to writing, Ed's been abusing other writers for several years at *Bewildering Stories*, where he serves on the review board and manages a posse of nine review editors. Ed is an active member of several writing groups, including the Fairfield Scribes, and the Poets' Salon, where he's known for his tough-love comments. He is also lead editor for the *Fairfield Scribes Micro Fiction* journal.

He has his original wife, but advises that after fifty some years together they are both out of warranty. Two children and five grandchildren serve as affection focus and money drain.

His writing began with a degree in journalism from the University of Illinois. Ed's career thereafter has been an enjoyably demented hopscotch game. U.S. Navy officer (diver and bomb disarmer); reporter for the *Providence Journal*; intelligence officer living in Germany and Japan; international sales and marketing executive at a North American paper company (twenty-three years, seventy four countries visited, MBA from NYU); eight more years as a sales executive for the company that also owns the New England Patriots; and retirement into writing like hell to make up for lost time.

www.ingramcontent.com/pod-product-compliance
Lightning Source LLC
Chambersburg PA
CBHW022127090426
42743CB00008B/1042